Original title:
Passion's Palette

Copyright © 2024 Book Fairy Publishing
All rights reserved.

Author: Marlen Vesiroos
ISBN HARDBACK: 978-9916-87-086-0
ISBN PAPERBACK: 978-9916-87-087-7

Spectrum of Secrets

In shadows dance the whispers low,
Secrets wrapped in layers slow.
Colors bleed from dark to light,
Hidden truths emerge from night.

Beneath the surface, silence churns,
Unspoken tales the heart still yearns.
Each hue a fragment of the soul,
A spectrum vast, we seek to whole.

Fingers trace where memories cling,
In every tone, a silent ring.
From violet dreams to crimson fears,
Our secrets swell, despite the years.

Let vibrance speak where words may fail,
Each shade a story, soft and frail.
As rainbows bridge the gaps we hide,
The spectrum sings where hearts reside.

Sunrise on the Canvas

Morning paints the world anew,
Brush of gold and softest blue.
Canvas stretched from sea to sky,
As dreams and light begin to fly.

Awakening the sleeping hues,
Whispers of a day to choose.
Pastel clouds, a gentle tease,
Awakening the silent trees.

Each dawn a promise, bright and bold,
Stories waiting to unfold.
In the light, our hopes ignite,
A dance of colors, pure delight.

Every stroke, a heartbeat's call,
On this canvas, we stand tall.
Sunrise bids the night goodbye,
And paints the dreams that never die.

Love's Vivid Narrative

In laughter's echo, love takes flight,
A vivid tale in soft twilight.
Each heartbeat marks a rhythm sweet,
With every glance, the world we meet.

Colors swirl in passion's dance,
Promises held in a fleeting glance.
Brush of hope, and stroke of trust,
In tender moments, love is just.

With every sigh, a story spun,
In quiet nights when day is done.
Each memory, a vibrant thread,
Woven tightly in what's said.

Through storms and sun, hand in hand,
Together, we will make our stand.
With vivid colors, hearts align,
In love's embrace, a world divine.

Reach for the Colors

In the sky where dreams take flight,
Reach for colors, bold and bright.
With every step, the world expands,
A canvas stretched by open hands.

Dance with shadows, spin in grace,
Find the hues that time won't chase.
Paint the moments, wild and free,
In every shade, the soul's decree.

Explore the edges where hopes arise,
In bursts of joy, let spirits rise.
Colors whisper in the breeze,
Awakening the heart with ease.

So take a chance, embrace the light,
In every hue, find pure delight.
Together, let our spirits soar,
And reach for colors evermore.

Palette of the Unseen

In shadows where whispers reside,
Colors dance, secrets collide.
A canvas brushed by twilight's hues,
Magic sparks where dreams diffuse.

Soft strokes blend in silent grace,
Invisible lines find their place.
Underneath the vibrant sky,
The unseen truths begin to cry.

Each tone holds a story untold,
Whispers of love, memoirs of old.
In the silence, they softly gleam,
Painting night with a waking dream.

Radiance in Motion

In the heart of the bustling day,
A burst of light finds its way.
Colors swirl like a gentle breeze,
Radiance buzzing through the leaves.

Every footstep ignites the ground,
Fleeting moments, joy unbound.
Shimmering threads weave through the air,
Breathless wonders, vibrant and rare.

As shadows dance with golden beams,
Life unfolds in glimmering dreams.
Together we chase, hand in hand,
A canvas bright, a painted land.

The Colors of Nostalgia

Faded pictures of days gone by,
Brushstrokes of laughter, a sweet sigh.
Golden hues of sunlit skies,
A palette rich with joyful cries.

Soft blues carry whispers of peace,
Memories linger, never cease.
Violet shades of twilight's call,
Recall the moments that once enthrall.

Crimson tones of love's embrace,
In every heart, they leave a trace.
Through the canvas of time we roam,
Each color leads us back home.

Prism of Tenderness

In the quiet folds of the night,
A prism bends soft beams of light.
Gentle whispers wrap around,
In every heart, love is found.

With each hue a feeling unfurls,
Tender moments like pearls and swirls.
Pastel shades of soft affection,
Coloring dreams in sweet reflection.

Through the glass, light softly flows,
Transforming pain to sweet repose.
In every glance, a silent vow,
A world reborn, here and now.

Tints of Treasures

In the morning light we find,
Colors whisper, soft and kind.
Each hue a secret, bright and bold,
Stories of treasures yet untold.

Golden rays dance on the sea,
Emerald leaves, wild and free.
Crimson sunsets set hearts ablaze,
Painting memories in a daze.

Blues like waves on distant shores,
Purple skies behind closed doors.
Every tint, a tale to weave,
Crafting dreams we dare believe.

With each brush of nature's hand,
We discover a hidden land.
A canvas rich with life and light,
Tints of treasures, pure delight.

Hues of Heartbeat

In the silence, colors bloom,
Softening shadows, brightening gloom.
With every pulse, they paint the air,
Whispers of love, a tender care.

Amber whispers of sweet refrain,
Rose petals brush away the pain.
In every heartbeat lies a spark,
Hues of hope in the dark.

A palette filled with dreams anew,
Brushstrokes light and colors true.
Violet nights and dawning gold,
A constant rhythm, bold and old.

Marigold mornings, fresh and bright,
Orange skies turn into night.
With every echo, we create,
Melodies that resonate.

Radiating Soul

From deep within the heart they rise,
Radiating warmth, like sunny skies.
The soul's essence, pure and clear,
In every shadow, it draws near.

Glistening like the stars above,
Tender whispers of endless love.
In every step, a spark ignites,
Radiating hope, winding lights.

Through twilight shades and dawn's embrace,
A journey traced in time and space.
Colors merging, intertwine,
Each thread a story, yours and mine.

Awakened dreams that softly glow,
In every moment, let it flow.
Radiate your truth, be free,
A shining beacon, just to be.

The Essence of Emotion

In the depth of silence, feelings swell,
The essence of emotion, a fragile spell.
A canvas brushed with laughter and tears,
Each stroke alive, reflecting our fears.

Joy blooms bright like spring's first breath,
Shadows linger, a dance with death.
In every tear, a river flows,
The essence of emotion, pure and close.

Echoes of sorrow, whispers of bliss,
Moments captured in an aching kiss.
Colors of longing, wild and free,
The essence of emotion, you and me.

Golden memories wrapped in time,
Singing softly in perfect rhyme.
Every heartbeat sings our song,
The essence of emotion, where we belong.

Chasing Fireflies

In the twilight glow, they dance,
Whispers of light, a fleeting chance.
Children laugh, their spirits soar,
In the garden, magic galore.

Bottles ready, we run and play,
Captured dreams, we keep at bay.
Flickering jewels in darkened night,
Nature's wonders, a pure delight.

Softly glowing, each little spark,
Guiding us through the endless dark.
Memories made with each gentle chase,
In the heart, we hold their grace.

As stars wane and dawn draws near,
The fireflies fade, yet disappear.
But echoes linger, sweet and bright,
Chasing dreams in soft twilight.

A fleeting moment, a tender sigh,
In the twilight, we learn to fly.
Enchanting beauty, forever cast,
In the heart, these fireflies last.

Hues of Ecstasy

Beneath the sun, a canvas blooms,
Colors burst, chasing the glooms.
Amber waves and azure skies,
Nature paints with no disguise.

Brushstrokes dance on rolling hills,
Awakening the dormant thrills.
Every petal, a story told,
In vibrant shades, both bright and bold.

Golden sunsets, whispers of day,
Crimson dreams chase blues away.
Glistening colors, a sweet embrace,
In this moment, we find our place.

Through stormy skies, the rain will fall,
Yet after, beauty conquers all.
An artist's heart, forever free,
In the hues of our ecstasy.

Life's vivid splash, our souls ignite,
In every shade, our shared delight.
Together we paint, forever strong,
In the chorus of colors, we belong.

The Color of Sensation

Emotions painted in vivid hues,
Each stroke a heartbeat, a vibrant muse.
Brushes of shadows, light dances and sways,
Capturing moments in a mosaic of days.

Textures of silence, the pulse of a sigh,
Nurtured by daylight, beneath a vast sky.
Every glance a canvas, each touch a refrain,
In this gallery of life, we find joy and pain.

Scent of a Dream

In the soft light of morning's glow,
Petals unfurl, a fragrant show.
Rose and jasmine, sweet and rare,
Whispers of dreams float in the air.

With each breath, memories wake,
A tapestry of love we make.
Nutmeg and vanilla entwined,
In every scent, our hearts aligned.

Golden fields, a warm embrace,
Nature's perfume, a sacred space.
The earth exudes its timeless grace,
In the scent, we find our place.

Quiet moments, drifting away,
In the essence of yesterday.
Every aroma, a cherished theme,
In the silence, we share a dream.

As dusk descends, we breathe in deep,
In twilight, secrets softly seep.
The scent of love forever stays,
In our hearts, a fragrant haze.

Palette of Shadows

In the midnight hour, whispers roam,
Silent echoes call us home.
Where shadows dance in moonlight's glow,
A palette rare, of ebb and flow.

Each dark hue tells a story deep,
In whispered secrets, silence we keep.
From charcoal nights to velvet dreams,
In shadowed corners, nothing's as it seems.

Beneath the stars, a canvas unfolds,
Mysteries cloaked in silken folds.
Flickers of hope through the despair,
In shadows, we wander, unafraid to dare.

The brush of night, both fierce and kind,
In shadows, lost treasures we find.
Through the darkness, we learn to see,
In hidden depths, we find the key.

With dawn's arrival, shadows fade,
Yet in our hearts, the colors made.
We carry forth, the stories told,
In the palette of shadows, brave and bold.

Drenched in Desire

In shadows of longing, we linger and play,
Each glance ignites fire, a burning ballet.
Fingers entwined, like vines in the sun,
In this tempestuous dance, we become one.

Whispers of silence, drenched in the heat,
Every heartbeat echoes a passionate beat.
The world fades away, just me and your gaze,
Lost in the moment, the passionate blaze.

The Canvas of Longing

Brush strokes whisper secrets,
A story of desire unfolds.
Each hue a fleeting moment,
In shadows, hope beholds.

Colors blend in quiet sorrow,
Palette dripped with tears.
An artist's heart feels hollow,
Reflecting all my fears.

Beneath the night's soft blanket,
Dreams dance in the dark.
A canvas holds my heartbeat,
Yearning for that spark.

The brush is my confessor,
In solitude I paint.
Each stroke, a deep confession,
Of love that feels so faint.

With every line and layering,
I craft my world anew.
In pigments of remembering,
Longing calls me through.

The Essence of Devotion

In whispered prayers, hearts entwine,
A promise made, your hand in mine.
Through stormy seas, our anchor stays,
In quiet moments, love's sweet praise.

With every glance, a spark ignites,
In shadows cast, our love takes flight.
In laughter shared, in tears we find,
The essence pure, our souls aligned.

A Symphony of Hues

In daylight's warm embrace,
Colors play, they twist and twine.
A symphony of hues,
Nature's own design.

Violet whispers softly,
Amidst the golden sun.
Emerald dreams await,
In dances, they have spun.

Cerulean skies above,
Reflect in waves below.
A melody of colors,
Where gentle breezes blow.

Crimson leaves in autumn,
Sway to the fading light.
A palette rich and vibrant,
Of day merging with night.

In this canvas breathing,
Life unfolds its tune.
A symphony that's fleeting,
Yet echoes with the moon.

Fire and Ink

With fire in my heart,
And ink upon the page,
I weave my thoughts in flames,
Defying every cage.

The words ignite like embers,
Sparking deep within.
Stories born from ashes,
Where shadows dare to grin.

Each verse a kindled whisper,
A dance of light and dark.
The ink bleeds into longing,
Leaving its tender mark.

In every line, a rescue,
From flames of doubt and fear.
The pen becomes a weapon,
As fire draws me near.

So I'll write through the twilight,
With passion as my guide.
Fire and ink together,
My spirit won't subside.

Tapestry of Dreams

In the loom of night, I weave,
Fingers dancing through the threads.
A tapestry of dreams,
Where magic softly spreads.

Stitches of bright laughter,
And shadows of despair.
Each fabric holds a whisper,
Of wishes made with care.

Colors clash and blend,
In this intricate design.
Every knot a story,
Every pattern, divine.

In twilight's gentle embrace,
I shape the tales I yearn.
Living in each moment,
For past and future learn.

A quilt of all my longings,
Sewn with threads of hope.
In this tapestry of dreams,
I find a way to cope.

Faded Sketches

Lines worn thin by time's embrace,
Shadows dance on paper's face.
Memories linger, soft and light,
Holding stories, out of sight.

Whispers of the past unfold,
Gentle tales, quietly told.
Ink that bleeds and starts to fade,
Echoes of a life once made.

Fragments stitched with tender care,
Fingers trace the vacant air.
Images that slowly die,
Leave their mark for us to sigh.

In the corners, dreams reside,
Fleeting moments, time's divide.
Each sketch breathes a silent plea,
To remember what used to be.

Faded colors, lost in haze,
Yet the heart still seeks to gaze.
On every line, a love bestowed,
In faded sketches, life once flowed.

Daring to Color Outside

Crayon dreams on borders bright,
Splashing hues that feel just right.
Stepping past the lines we know,
Where the wildest visions grow.

With every stroke, a chance we take,
In the chaos, new dreams wake.
Vivid shades of bold intent,
Unlocking joy where fear was spent.

Fearless heart and painted hands,
Crafting futures, making plans.
Every splash, a note of glee,
Channeling what's yet to be.

In the mess, we find our muse,
Colors merge, and paths we choose.
Through the noise, our spirits climb,
Creating art, defying time.

Daring leaps that set us free,
In the world, we paint our spree.
Drawing life in every shade,
Coloring outside—that's how it's made.

Mosaic of Affection

In a frame of whispers, we find our grace,
Each little moment, a tender embrace.
Colors of laughter dance on our skin,
In this mosaic, where love begins.

Fragments of stories, pieced with care,
Every heartbeat shared, a treasure rare.
Underneath the stars, our secrets spill,
A tapestry woven, both soft and still.

The Poetry of Touch

Fingers dance, a silent song,
In the fabric, where we belong.
Gentle tremors, soft and sweet,
Words unspoken, where hearts meet.

In the warmth of soft embrace,
Every brush ignites a flame.
Tender whispers, skin to skin,
Reveal the stories deep within.

Texture speaks in ways profound,
In each touch, a love is found.
Unraveled secrets, shared delight,
Breathe in shadows, hold them tight.

Glimmers of a shared refrain,
Each caress a sweet domain.
In the silence, volumes say,
The poetry we weave each day.

Every moment, lost in grace,
In the touch, we find our place.
Crafting verses with the heart,
In this dance, we'll never part.

Fluid Emotions

Rivers of feelings flow through the night,
Each wave a memory, lost to the light.
Drifting on currents, we ebb and we flow,
Transient moments, like whispers, we know.

A dance of our hearts, both heavy and free,
Caught in the tides of what's yet to be.
Waves crashing softly on rocks, they collide,
In the vast ocean, where secrets reside.

A Dabble in Desire

Whispers linger in the night,
Flickering, soft candlelight.
Eyes that glimmer, souls that yearn,
In the fire, passions burn.

Every heartbeat sings a song,
In this place, we both belong.
Tangled dreams that intertwine,
In the hush, our hopes align.

Fingers trace the hidden curves,
In each touch, the tension swerves.
A sweet tension, pulsing strong,
Guiding us where we belong.

Words unspoken, breathless sighs,
Painting stars within our eyes.
In this moment, wild and free,
Desire's dance is meant to be.

A fleeting glance, the world turns slow,
With a spark, our passions grow.
In this dabble, love's embrace,
We find our home, our resting place.

Eclectic Elation

In laughter's glow, we find our way,
Dancing shadows, night and day.
Colors swirling, a vivid spree,
Together we paint our destiny.

Moments sparkle, like stars on high,
With every heartbeat, we touch the sky.
Elation bursts, a joyful refrain,
In this tapestry, love is our gain.

Melodies rise, a symphony bright,
Whispers of dreams, taking flight.
In the chaos, stillness resides,
Eclectic hearts, where joy abides.

Through every challenge, we embrace,
Finding beauty in every space.
United we stand, steadfast and bold,
In the warmth of laughter, our story unfolds.

So here's to the moments, pure and true,
In the dance of life, it's me and you.
Together we'll weave our splendid tale,
Eclectic elation, let it prevail.

Chiaroscuro of Love

In shadows deep, where secrets lie,
Two souls converge, as time slips by.
With gentle whispers, truths unfold,
In the chiaroscuro, love is bold.

The light and dark, they intertwine,
In every heartbeat, a design.
Through trials faced, our spirits soar,
In contrast found, we love much more.

Colors in Collision

Brush strokes vivid, passion unleashed,
A canvas alive, beauty increased.
Crimson and azure, bold and bright,
In colors colliding, day turns to night.

Splashes of dreams, like rain in June,
Echoes of laughter, a playful tune.
Artists at heart, we paint our fate,
In every hue, we celebrate.

The world ignites with each vibrant shade,
In the gallery of life, memories made.
Fusion of feelings, a splendid array,
Colors colliding, guide our way.

With every stroke, emotions flow,
In the chaos, a rhythm to show.
We dance through the shades, intertwined,
In this masterpiece, our souls aligned.

So let the colors run wild and free,
In the heart of creation, just you and me.
Together we'll blend a spectrum bright,
A canvas of love, our guiding light.

Heartbeat of a Masterpiece

In every heartbeat, a story is spun,
Threads of existence, woven as one.
Each pulse a note in a timeless song,
A masterpiece born, where we belong.

The canvas waits, with colors unspoken,
Moments captured, never broken.
With gentle strokes, the vision unfolds,
A symphony painted, as daylight holds.

Emotions flutter, like leaves in the breeze,
With every heartbeat, we find our ease.
Under the stars, dreams intertwine,
In the whispers of night, our souls align.

Crafting our fate with delicate grace,
Through trials and triumphs, we find our place.
In the gallery of time, where memories roam,
The heartbeat of love, our eternal home.

So let's create, with passion ablaze,
A masterpiece born of joy and praise.
With every heartbeat, our art will thrive,
In the canvas of life, we are alive.

The Artistry of Yearning

In the silence, longing takes flight,
Whispers of dreams, dancing in light.
A brush in hand, we sketch the skies,
With colors dripping from our sighs.

Through twilight shadows, desires weave,
The artistry of yearning, we believe.
Every stroke tells a tale untold,
In the heart's gallery, treasures unfold.

With every heartbeat, we chase the flame,
In the realm of hope, we stake our claim.
The canvas stretches, wide and vast,
A legacy born from futures and past.

With gentle hues, we paint the pain,
Transforming anguish into gain.
In every layer, depth is found,
In the artistry of longing, we're unbound.

So let the yearnings reach for the stars,
In vibrant colors, forget the scars.
Together we'll craft this vivid dream,
The artistry of yearning, a radiant theme.

Notes of Colorful Whimsy

In gardens bright with hues that sing,
Wanders imagination on gentle wing.
A splash of laughter in the breeze,
Whispers secrets among the trees.

Dancing petals twirl and sway,
Drawing joy from night and day.
Each color tells a story clear,
Echoing dreams that linger near.

In every shade, a tale unfurls,
The magic flows, it twirls and whirls.
Across the canvas, life takes flight,
A tapestry of pure delight.

An artist's heart, a child's play,
Fleeting moments, bright array.
With every brush, a world anew,
A symphony in vibrant hue.

So let us play in fields of grace,
Where whimsy holds a timeless space.
In laughter's note and joy's embrace,
We find our truth, our perfect place.

The Stroke of Serendipity

A chance encounter in the sun,
Where two hearts meet, together run.
A laugh, a smile, a spark ignites,
In moments fleeting, joy ignites.

Like brush on canvas, strokes of fate,
Paths intertwine, it feels so great.
In whispered winds, our stories blend,
A gentle touch, a newfound friend.

The universe conspires so,
To push and pull, to ebb and flow.
In every glance, a cosmic thread,
Leads us onward, where hope is spread.

Colors swirling in the night,
A tapestry of purest light.
With every chance, a dance begins,
In serendipity, where love wins.

So here we stand, two souls aligned,
In this sweet moment, joy defined.
Forever changed by fate's kind hand,
In the magic of this land.

Threads of Obsession

In silent rooms where shadows creep,
Threads of obsession weaves so deep.
A flicker here, a whisper there,
Tangled thoughts, a lover's snare.

With every glance, a burning fire,
A pulsing need that won't retire.
In tangled yarns of passion's hue,
We find ourselves, entwined, anew.

Night stars flicker, the world fades,
In this labyrinth, our hearts cascade.
Together caught in fevered schemes,
Chasing echoes of forgotten dreams.

In gentle pulls, our spirits yearn,
For every twist, there's much to learn.
Through threads that bind, we grasp the light,
In obsessions' dance, we take our flight.

So tread with care, yet do not fear,
For love's sweet thread will draw us near.
In fibers woven, we will stay,
In this obsession, find our way.

A Dance with Color

In twilight hours, the colors play,
Dancing together, night and day.
With every twirl, a story spun,
In vibrant shades, we come undone.

With reds like roses, bold and bright,
Yellows flicker, bringing light.
Blues like oceans, deep and wide,
Whispering secrets, hearts abide.

Together we weave a vibrant dream,
Colors merge, in bliss we gleam.
Amidst this dance, we lose our cares,
In strokes of laughter, love declares.

Every hue, a heart's release,
With every step, we find our peace.
In this dance, we shall explore,
The beauty of life, forevermore.

So let us sway, let spirits rise,
With colors bright, beneath the skies.
In a dance with color, we are free,
A celebration of you and me.

Radiant Reveries

In twilight's glow, dreams take flight,
Whispers of stars in the soft night.
Every shadow dances softly here,
Painting the sky with our quiet cheer.

Moments linger, sweet and bright,
Chasing the echoes of fleeting light.
In the stillness, heartbeats blend,
A tapestry woven, no need to mend.

Gentle breezes hum a tune,
Softly guiding beneath the moon.
In this space, time stands still,
Filling our souls with a timeless thrill.

Each memory glimmers, pure and clear,
Filled with laughter and tender cheer.
In radiant dreams we find our way,
Sunrise will come to light our day.

As dawn breaks in hues, warm and bold,
The story of us gently unfolds.
In reveries bright, we take our stand,
With hope in our hearts, we walk hand in hand.

Infusion of Urgency

The clock ticks loud, a hurried sound,
Each moment lost can't be found.
In the heat of chase, we're alive,
With every heartbeat, we strive to thrive.

The city pulses, energy flows,
A rush of life wherever it goes.
In crowded streets, we weave and dart,
A tapestry woven from each brave heart.

Fear lingers close, yet we push on,
Chasing the dawn before it's gone.
Adrenaline surges, igniting our fire,
In every challenge lies our desire.

Moments ignite like matches strobed,
With sparks of courage, we're boldly probed.
Through walls of doubt, we burst and rise,
With every struggle, new strength supplies.

So let this urgency fill our veins,
Creating paths through struggles and pains.
In every heartbeat, there's a call,
To live more fiercely, to risk it all.

Emotions Run Wild

In the heart's depth, feelings surge,
Like wild rivers, they twist and merge.
Joy and sorrow, hand in hand,
Creating a symphony, strong and grand.

Sunlit moments spark delight,
As shadows whisper through the night.
Every tear, a story unfolds,
In the dance of life, our truth beholds.

With laughter loud, we break the chains,
In this chaos, love remains.
Every heartbeat echoes clear,
Through tangled paths, we persevere.

Emotions ebbed, then flowed anew,
Crafting colors in every hue.
With open arms, we face the tide,
Finding strength where dreams reside.

In moments fleeting, we find our grace,
Within wild feelings, we find our place.
Emotions run wild, fierce and true,
In the fabric of life, we weave anew.

Painted Desires

With brush in hand, we stroke the sky,
Each color blends as dreams come by.
In whispers soft, desires glow,
Creating visions only we know.

The canvas stretches, wide and free,
Holding wishes like whispers of a plea.
In vibrant hues, our hearts take flight,
Painting the day, igniting the night.

As shadows linger, colors shift,
A dance of longing, a timeless gift.
Each splash and swirl, a story told,
Within painted desires, our futures unfold.

Dark strokes blend with shades of light,
Crafting the path where dreams ignite.
In every stroke, a hope revealed,
A masterpiece waiting to be sealed.

So let us wander, brush in hand,
Across this landscape, vast and grand.
With painted desires, we leave our mark,
In the gallery of life, we'll spark.

Whispers of Color

In the garden where dreams unfold,
Petals whisper secrets, bright and bold.
Crimson and gold, a vibrant display,
Nature's palette paints the day.

Breezes carry scents so sweet,
Dancing leaves in rhythmic beat.
Each hue tells a tale of grace,
A vivid tapestry we embrace.

Morning dew on emerald blades,
Sunlight glimmers, softly invades.
Colors bloom in gentle light,
Awakening hearts, taking flight.

Savory shades, both dark and light,
Life's canvas reveals pure delight.
With every stroke, a story unfolds,
In whispers of color, beauty holds.

The Dance of Desire

Under the moon's watchful gaze,
Hearts entwined in a fevered blaze.
Whispers exchanged, bodies align,
In the night, their spirits entwine.

Fingers trace the outline of dreams,
Electric sparks and silken seams.
Passion ignites like blazing fire,
Every heartbeat fuels desire.

Between the shadows, they sway,
Lost in each other, come what may.
A dance of souls, unspoken art,
The rhythm beats within their hearts.

With every glance, the world fades away,
In the moment, they long to stay.
Through the dark, their bodies move,
In this dance, they find their groove.

In layers of longing, they dive deep,
Secrets shared are theirs to keep.
Every pull, every playful tease,
An endless tango, seeking to please.

Brushstrokes of Emotion

On canvas wide, feelings spill,
Vivid hues that time can't kill.
Every brushstroke tells a tale,
Of joy and sorrow that prevail.

With colors bold, fears are faced,
Life's complexities interlaced.
A splash of blue for days gone wrong,
And strokes of yellow, bright, and strong.

In the quiet, whispers blend,
Art transcends, it can mend.
From shadows deep, light will burst,
Emotions expressed, quenching thirst.

Each layer reveals a hidden part,
A glimpse of the soul, a work of heart.
Through vibrant strokes, we find reprieve,
In brushstrokes of emotion, we believe.

With every hue, memories dance,
Inviting hope, igniting chance.
In every stroke, life flows free,
An artist's heart spills its decree.

Shades of Love's Embrace

In twilight's glow, two shadows merge,
A sacred bond, pure hearts surge.
Soft whispers drift on evening air,
In love's embrace, they find their prayer.

Gentle touches, tender glances,
Lost in the rhythm of sweet romances.
Every heartbeat echoes a song,
Together is where they truly belong.

Through storms and sun, hand in hand,
They navigate this promised land.
With every smile, shades entwined,
In love's embrace, their souls aligned.

Seasons change, yet their fire burns,
In life's embrace, each lesson learns.
Through trials faced, their passion stays,
In shades of love, they spend their days.

In moments captured, forever framed,
A tapestry of love reclaimed.
In each embrace, a world's set free,
In shades of love's embrace, they see.

Ardent Whispers

In the quiet night we speak,
Soft murmurs in the dark,
Hearts aflame, feelings peak,
Igniting every spark.

Dreams drift like morning mist,
In the glow of moonlit skies,
Promises sealed with a kiss,
Underneath the stars' sighs.

Time slows when you are near,
A world within our grasp,
Each sweet laugh I hold dear,
In this love, I gladly clasp.

Winds carry words profound,
Whispers of the heart's grace,
In this magic we have found,
Eternity's warm embrace.

The night will never fade,
In your arms, I long to stay,
With ardent whispers made,
We chase the dawn's first ray.

Canvas of Connection

Brush strokes of vibrant hue,
Mingled with shades of the past,
Each line tells a tale true,
Moments we've made to last.

Colors blend in sweet embrace,
Creating a masterpiece,
Every shade finds its place,
In the art of our peace.

Canvas stretched beneath the sun,
Splashing joy on life's page,
A journey just begun,
With you, I'll never age.

Textures rise, emotions flow,
With every heartbeat, we dare,
In this gallery, love will grow,
Connecting souls laid bare.

At dusk, we paint the night,
Stars joining our vivid dance,
In this canvas, pure delight,
Together, we take a chance.

Palette of Pulses

Rhythms beat within the soul,
A symphony of our hearts,
Each thrum plays a vital role,
In this world, where love starts.

Life's colors swirl and dive,
In the slow, sweet embrace,
Our spirits fully alive,
Lost in time, in this space.

With every pulse, we collide,
Movement painting the air,
In this dance, love won't hide,
Connection beyond compare.

Now we draw from deep below,
Notes of laughter, echoes clear,
Creating a vibrant flow,
Within us, we hold dear.

Together, we find our way,
In the music of our song,
Holding tight to what we say,
In this pulse, we belong.

Whirling Around the Sun

Time spins in a golden thread,
Circled by the dawn's bright light,
In this dance, we're daily fed,
By warmth that chases the night.

Planets swirl in cosmic grace,
We twirl, lost in love's embrace,
Each heartbeat a timeless trace,
Holding dreams, our special place.

Days blend in the softest hues,
As shadows stretch and fade,
In this world we both choose,
Wonders of life displayed.

Through seasons, we spin and glide,
With laughter guiding our way,
Together, let's take the ride,
In this dance, where we will stay.

Whirling around our own sun,
In moments of shared delight,
In our orbit, we are one,
Chasing ever after light.

Shades of an Undying Flame

In the heart of the night, it glows,
Catching whispers the darkness knows.
A flicker of hope in a sea of despair,
Its warmth a promise, forever rare.

Dancing shadows, they twist and sway,
Fleeting moments that fade away.
Yet in its light, secrets revealed,
Stories of longing, softly concealed.

Embers flicker, a soft embrace,
Each glow a memory, each spark a trace.
Through the silence, it softly calls,
A beacon alive as the night falls.

In every spark, a tale to tell,
Of laughter and tears, of heaven and hell.
An undying flame, vibrant and true,
In shadows it lives, in colors anew.

So let it burn, let it shine bright,
Through the darkness, it is our light.
A promise that lingers, a fire untamed,
In shades of passion, forever named.

Painting the Night

The canvas stretches, vast and wide,
Stars like brushstrokes, side by side.
With every shimmer, the night unfolds,
A tale of magic in colors bold.

Azure skies meet twilight's hue,
Whispers of dusk in shades of blue.
The moon, a palette, glimmers bright,
Casting dreams in the cloak of night.

Each stroke a memory, soft and clear,
Blending hopes with visions near.
The shadows dance in quiet delight,
Painting stories in the gentle night.

Silhouettes swirl in the midnight air,
Echoes of love and tender care.
In this realm, hearts unite,
Crafting beauty when painting the night.

As dawn approaches, colors will fade,
Yet the heart's canvas will never jade.
For in every moment, we find our way,
In the art of living, come what may.

Rhapsody in Hue

An orchestra woven with shades of light,
Each color a note, taking flight.
The symphony plays through shadowed trees,
Whispering secrets in the breeze.

Crimson passion ignites the dawn,
Turquoise dreams carry us on.
With every blend, a story flows,
In rhapsody where the heart knows.

Golden gleams of the setting sun,
A harmony played, never done.
Violet whispers of peace surround,
In this masterpiece, love is found.

Every stroke, a different tune,
Painting the world, morning to moon.
In the palette of life, we all sway,
In rhapsody of hue, come what may.

So let the colors swirl and dance,
In this vibrant life, take a chance.
For each moment matters, vivid and true,
In the rhapsody of a world anew.

Illusions of Intensity

In the depths where colors collide,
Illusions of joy and fears abide.
Every hue a tale half-told,
Echoes of fervor, young and old.

Bright flames flicker, shadows play,
Mirages of hope that drift away.
Within the heart, intensity dreams,
Alluring whispers in moonlit beams.

The vibrant dance of striking shades,
Fleeting moments that never fade.
Passion ignites in the sacred night,
Illusions shimmer, elusive light.

Yet in the depths, the truth does lie,
In every color that captures the eye.
Through the haze, we see, we feel,
The depth of pain, the joy, the real.

For in the contrast, beauty can bloom,
Illusions fading, banishing gloom.
A canvas alive where shadows play,
In the heart of colors, we find our way.

Echoes in Watercolors

Beneath the skies of pastel light,
Ripples dance with soft delight,
Brush strokes whisper, tales to weave,
In the stillness, hearts believe.

Colors merge in gentle sway,
Memories float like clouds at play,
A canvas bright, no shadows cast,
Echoes of moments, fading fast.

Each droplet holds a silent song,
Where dreams and hopes are never wrong,
In vibrant hues, the past is found,
Life's rhythm flows, a tender sound.

With every splash, a secret shared,
In watercolor, souls are bared,
Captured in hues, forever bright,
Together, we embrace the light.

In twilight's glow, reflections gleam,
A masterpiece born from a dream,
Echoes linger, soft and low,
In watercolors, love will grow.

Varnished Hopes

In a world where dreams are sealed,
Varnished hopes are gently revealed,
Glittering under the sun's embrace,
Every shimmer has its place.

Polished wishes line the shelf,
Crafted with care by hands oneself,
Each layer tells of battles fought,
In the silence, wisdom's sought.

Hues of longing blend with cheer,
A tapestry of joy and fear,
Glistening bright, yet worn with time,
In varnished hopes, we find our rhyme.

Dreams hang like ornaments bright,
Reflecting shadows of the night,
We polish them with every goal,
Building bridges for the soul.

With every stroke, new stories born,
Varnished hopes, never worn,
Together we shine, unafraid to cope,
In the heart of our faith, a glimmer of hope.

Color-Craze

Splashes of life swirl and sway,
In the heart of a color-craze,
Every hue, a tale to tell,
Dancing in joy, we know so well.

Crimson dreams and azure skies,
Paint our days with sweet surprise,
Emerald whispers, golden light,
In this canvas, we find delight.

A riot of colors, bold and free,
Unleashing wild creativity,
Every shade a heartbeat's drum,
A world where art and passion hum.

Through every stroke, a story spins,
A tapestry where life begins,
Color-craze wraps, a warm embrace,
Uniting hearts in sacred space.

In vivid dreams, we leap and play,
In this color-craze, come what may,
With laughter bright and spirits high,
We paint the joy across the sky.

Hearts in Bloom

In the garden where dreams arise,
Hearts in bloom, beneath the skies,
Petals open, soft and true,
Each whisper holds the morning dew.

Colors twine in fragrant air,
A symphony of love laid bare,
With every bud, a promise spins,
New beginnings, where life begins.

In sunlight's kiss, we find our way,
Through shadows cast at end of day,
Hearts entwined in nature's grace,
In blooms, we find our sacred space.

With vibrant strokes, our stories blend,
Each flower tells where hearts transcend,
Together we grow, roots entwined,
In this tapestry, love defined.

As seasons change, and blossoms fade,
In memories, we are not afraid,
For in each bloom, a piece of light,
Hearts in bloom, forever bright.

Chasing the Horizon

Beneath the vast and open sky,
The sun sets low, the day says bye.
With dreams like stars, we venture forth,
Chasing the light that brings us worth.

Each step we take on untamed ground,
In whispers soft, the hope is found.
Through fields of gold and shadows fine,
We reach for worlds beyond the line.

The ocean's edge calls out our name,
In waves that crash, we stake our claim.
The horizon beckons with a song,
In endless dance, we both belong.

With every breath, we touch the sky,
Where dreams ignite and spirits fly.
No longer tethered to the past,
We chase the horizon, free at last.

And when the night enfolds the day,
We'll find our peace in starlit sway.
For in the chase, our hearts ignite,
Together always, we shine bright.

Caressing the Canvas

Gentle strokes of vibrant hue,
A world awakens, fresh and new.
With every brush, a tale unfolds,
In whispers soft, the canvas holds.

Colors blend and dance with ease,
Each stroke a sigh, a silent breeze.
With sunlit gold and ocean blue,
The heart spills out, a dream come true.

A splash of red, a hint of green,
In every shade, a life unseen.
The canvas breathes, it starts to glow,
As visions formed begin to flow.

With passion fierce, we create and mold,
A silent story waiting to be told.
In every line, our spirits roam,
As we caress the canvas home.

And when the colors fade to night,
We'll hold the art, our pure delight.
For in this space, our dreams explore,
In every stroke, we seek for more.

Tints Beyond the Horizon

Past the edge where colors blend,
Lies a world that knows no end.
In tints of pink and shades of blue,
Awaits a life, both bright and true.

With every dawn, the colors rise,
A canvas vast beneath the skies.
The sun's embrace, the moon's soft glow,
In tints beyond, our spirits flow.

Each shade a promise, each hue a song,
In whispers sweet, where dreams belong.
With every touch, we break the mold,
The heart's true story, brave and bold.

Through valleys deep and mountains high,
We seek the tints that catch the eye.
In every moment, life displayed,
With colors bright, our fears allayed.

And when the day turns into night,
We'll find the stars, our guiding light.
For in the tints, the world we see,
Awaits a journey, wild and free.

Elysian Artistry

In realms where beauty breathes and sighs,
Each moment crafted, pure surprise.
With hands that shape, with hearts that care,
We find our art in love laid bare.

The palette rich, the canvas wide,
In every stroke, our dreams reside.
From darkest depths to light divine,
Elysian grace in every line.

With every curve, each form we mold,
A story told, a truth unrolled.
Through colors bright and shadows cast,
Eternal whispers linger last.

In sacred spaces, hearts collide,
With passion fierce, we set aside
The doubts that cloud, the fears that bind,
In artistry, our souls unwind.

And when the final piece is shown,
We'll find our joy in all we've grown.
For in this craft, we seek to trust,
In Elysian artistry, we must.

Vivid Flames of Yearning

In shadows deep where passions glow,
Desires dance like fire's flow.
Each flicker tells a secret rare,
A longing whispered in the air.

Through nights adorned with silken dreams,
Heartbeats echo, silent screams.
Embers warm the coldest nights,
Yearning sparks in swirling lights.

With every wave of pulsing tides,
Hopes ignited where truth confides.
A blaze that wanes yet never dies,
In vivid hues the spirit flies.

The canvas holds our fervent wish,
In painted strokes we find our bliss.
A fire within, forever stirs,
In vivid flames, our hearts concur.

So let the embers softly speak,
Of fervent dreams, of love so meek.
In every blaze our souls entwine,
In yearning's dance, we find the sign.

Chromatic Heartstrings

With every hue, a tale unfolds,
In tangled threads, the heart beholds.
Colors weave through time and space,
A vibrant tune of warm embrace.

Scarlet echoes of sweet romance,
Indigo whispers in a trance.
Golden rays of laughter ring,
While azure skies of hope take wing.

In palettes bright our stories blend,
Melodies that twist and bend.
A symphony of shades alive,
In chromatic joy, we thrive.

Each stroke a memory, a sigh,
Fragrant blooms where feelings lie.
Crafted moments, vivid, bold,
In heartstrings strummed, our lives unfold.

Let's paint our world in vibrant dreams,
Where every color softly gleams.
Together in this artful play,
Our souls rejoice, come what may.

The Art of Affection

In gentle brush strokes, love takes flight,
A canvas pure, of day and night.
With whispers soft, we share our truth,
In every glance, we find our youth.

From tender words, a portrait grows,
Each laugh a stroke that glows and flows.
A masterpiece of hearts combined,
In every gesture, love defined.

With open arms, we shape our fate,
In secret smiles, we celebrate.
The brush of time, the hues of grace,
In every heartbeat, we embrace.

The stories told in colors bright,
In shadows cast, we find the light.
Together, we refine the art,
Of affection shared, from heart to heart.

In this gallery of dreams we roam,
With every stroke, we build our home.
The art of love in every line,
Forever cherished, sweet and divine.

Brush of Ecstasy

With every stroke, life starts to sing,
In colors bold, the joy they bring.
A dance of shades, a sweet embrace,
With passion drawn, we find our place.

The brush it glides on canvas wide,
Revealing all we try to hide.
A touch of bliss in every hue,
In ecstasy, we start anew.

Each line expresses what words can't share,
A dance of spirits hanging air.
The world transformed through vibrant dreams,
In artful strokes, our longing beams.

Electric moments caught in time,
A symphony, our souls entwined.
The brush it tells what hearts conceal,
Through ecstasy, our truths reveal.

In every color, life ignites,
A blaze of passion, pure delights.
Together in this playful trance,
With brush of ecstasy, we dance.

Cherished Strokes

With each gentle touch, colors dance,
In a canvas alive, dreams take their chance.
Whispers of joy, in each stroke we lay,
A memory captured, never to fray.

The heart sings softly, as hues intertwine,
Moments immortalized, so sweet, so divine.
Brush in hand, souls begin to unfold,
A story of love, vivid and bold.

Each layer a treasure, a tale to be told,
Of laughter and tears, of warmth and of cold.
Through cherished strokes, we find our way,
In a world of art, forever we'll stay.

Art breathes life into silence and space,
Each curve and each line, a lover's embrace.
With a palette of dreams, we paint the night,
In our cherished strokes, everything feels right.

Together we create, bound by desire,
A tapestry woven, setting hearts on fire.
Through every canvas, our spirits ignite,
In cherished strokes, we find pure delight.

Curves of Curiosity

Curves that beckon, stories unfold,
In the dance of existence, we become bold.
Each twist and turn, a whisper, a tease,
Drawn to the unknown, a heart seeks to please.

Waves of wonder, in every embrace,
Each curve a journey, a sacred space.
Questions like shadows, trailing behind,
In curves of curiosity, the answers we find.

Through valleys of thought, we wander, we roam,
In the labyrinth of life, we carve our own home.
Chasing the edges, the soft and the steep,
In the curves of curiosity, secrets we keep.

Floating on dreams, we venture afar,
Guided by starlight, each radiant star.
In the arcs of existence, we feel so alive,
With curves of curiosity, together we thrive.

The dance of the curious, so wild and free,
In every heartbeat, there's more to see.
Together we wander, hand in hand,
In curves of curiosity, forever we stand.

The Brush That Binds

A brush dipped in dreams, colors collide,
In each gentle stroke, our hearts open wide.
With every embrace, a story is spun,
The brush that binds us, two souls become one.

From light to the dark, we journey through time,
Creating a rhythm, a sweet, silent rhyme.
With whispers of love, we paint the night sky,
The brush that binds us, teaching us to fly.

Each hue tells a tale, of laughter and tears,
With strokes of affection, we conquer our fears.
In layers of color, our voices combine,
Through the brush that binds, forever we shine.

With every creation, we find a new home,
In the world of our art, we'll never roam alone.
The brush in our hands, a magical gift,
A force that empowers, our spirits to lift.

In the dance of creation, our spirits entwined,
In the art we create, our souls are aligned.
The brush that binds, a sweet legacy shared,
In every stroke, a love that has dared.

Layers of Love

Beneath the surface, emotions reside,
In layers of love, where secrets can hide.
Still waters run deep, passions fulfill,
A journey of hearts, forever we will.

Textured like silk, each layer a blend,
Of moments collected, where beginnings transcend.
With patience we brush, with kindness we weave,
In layers of love, we dare to believe.

The more we uncover, the more we embrace,
With colors of friendship, we paint every space.
In twilight's soft glow, our stories will shine,
In layers of love, your heart melds with mine.

Every heartbeat whispers, a promise, a vow,
In layers of love, we're anchored and wowed.
Together we build, a world so divine,
With each tender layer, our spirits entwine.

In the art of our love, we've found our true song,
In layers that flourish, we've learned we belong.
With every new color, our canvas expands,
In layers of love, forever we stand.

Harmonies in Hue

Whispers of dawn bring soft light,
Colors blend in morning's flight.
Crimson dances with shades of blue,
Nature sings in every hue.

Golden rays kiss the dew's glow,
Painting fields where wildflowers grow.
Lilacs sway in the gentle breeze,
Carried forth with such sweet ease.

In twilight's arms, the canvas shimmers,
Obsidian skies with silver glimmers.
Each shade a note in the evening song,
Together they play, where all belong.

With every hue, a story spun,
A tapestry woven by the sun.
In each layer, life's pulse flows,
In harmonies of colors, it grows.

From vibrant reds to softest pastels,
In every pigment, a secret dwells.
Embrace the beauty, let it renew,
In the dance of life's vivid view.

Surrender to the Spectrum

Under the veil of twilight's embrace,
Colors collide in a mystic space.
Let go of shadows, let worries cease,
In the spectrum's arms, find your peace.

Radiant hues swirl like a dream,
A cascade of light in a flowing stream.
Vortex of thoughts, gently unwind,
In this kaleidoscope, freedom you'll find.

Each color a whisper, a soft refrain,
Echoing truths amidst the pain.
Surrender the heart, let it ignite,
In the spectrum's glow, embrace the light.

From fiery oranges to emerald green,
Each shade a story, each stroke serene.
Feel the rush as you dive deep,
In the sea of colors, let your soul leap.

In the twilight hues, find solace anew,
Surrender to the spectrum, let life ensue.
With every brush, create your tale,
In vibrant strokes where spirits sail.

Merging Melodies

Notes rise softly like morning mist,
In the air, sweet sounds twist.
Melodies weave through sunlit trees,
An orchestra played by the gentle breeze.

Harmony flows in tandem today,
Rhythms merge in a waltzing sway.
Strings and winds, a dance align,
Creating a song, divine and fine.

Chords collide, a serendipitous fate,
Each note a step to a grander state.
Resonate deeply, let the hearts sing,
In this symphony, life takes wing.

In every whisper, the echoes sound,
In every heartbeat, music is found.
Let whispers of love fill the air,
In joining this dance, we all can share.

As dusk descends, the harmonies swell,
Uniting the stories we cherish and tell.
In merging melodies, we find our part,
A rhythm that flows from the depths of the heart.

Creations of the Heart

From the depths where emotions rise,
Crafting dreams beneath the skies.
Every vision a spark, ignited bright,
In the canvas of the soul, pure light.

Whispers of hopes take vibrant form,
Each creation born from the storm.
In the palette of love, colors flow,
Painting tales we long to show.

Brush strokes dance in delicate grace,
Capturing time in a timeless space.
Fleeting moments made eternal,
In the heart's echo, truths infernal.

Sculpting shadows, giving them breath,
Creating beauty, defying death.
In every heartbeat, a story unfolds,
In creations of the heart, life beholds.

Artistry flows like a river knows,
In each gentle curve, the spirit grows.
Inviting all to feel and see,
In this gallery of the heart, we are free.

A Symphony in Oil

Brush strokes dance upon the canvas,
Colors swirl in a gentle embrace,
A tale of passion, bold and vivid,
Each hue sings in its rightful place.

Whispers of life in every layer,
Textures breathe with fervent delight,
From shadows deep to highlights glowing,
An orchestra composed in light.

The artist's heart spills on the surface,
With each gesture, dreams come alive,
In this gallery of emotions,
Where imagination will always thrive.

Moments caught in a fleeting vision,
The palette reflects the soul's desire,
In every painting, a new story,
That ignites the artist's inner fire.

As the world fades behind this doorway,
The spirit dances, wild and free,
In a symphony of colors and passions,
Art becomes the language of the sea.

The Heart's Bloom

In the garden where dreams awaken,
Petals open to the morning sun,
Fragrance sweetens the gentle breezes,
A love story waiting to be spun.

Dewdrops glisten like whispers soft,
Each blossom tells of moments held,
In vibrant shades of red and gold,
Their secrets in the sunlight swelled.

Beneath the branches, hearts entwined,
Two souls dance in nature's embrace,
With every laugh, the roses flourish,
In this tranquil, sacred space.

Seasons change, yet love endures,
Through autumn's chill and winter's frost,
Springs ignorance is gently broken,
For the heart knows not what is lost.

As petals fall to the skin of earth,
A cycle begins, ever new,
In every end, there lies a promise,
The heart's bloom will always renew.

Colorful Secrets Unveiled

Behind the curtain, shadows linger,
A vibrant world waits to be seen,
Colors clash and whisper softly,
In a dance, both fierce and serene.

The canvas hides its whispered tales,
A spectrum of dreams and delight,
With each brushstroke, secrets awaken,
A vibrant tapestry takes flight.

Diverse palettes mingle and swirl,
As the artist pours forth their heart,
Each layer holds a hidden meaning,
A journey where worlds drift apart.

In the eyes of those who behold,
These colorful secrets softly speak,
With every hue, a story unfolds,
In silence, the heart seeks the meek.

As the final touch graces the painting,
A moment captured in pure bliss,
The secrets emerge, vibrant and bold,
In their colors, the world finds its kiss.

The Art of Infatuation

In every glance, the spark ignites,
A longing wrapped in sweet disguise,
With whispered words and lingering sighs,
The art of love, a dance of bites.

Fleeting moments, stolen hours,
A blush that blooms with every glance,
Swept away in this fevered state,
Each heartbeat sings a siren's dance.

Brush the fingertips, electric thrill,
As time stands still in tender arms,
With every kiss, a canvas born,
In silent promises and half-formed charms.

Caught in the web of fleeting dreams,
Where fantasy and reality blend,
Navigating through uncharted waters,
With every heartbeat, the chase extends.

As the colors fade and moments wane,
The echo lingers, soft and sweet,
In the art of infatuation's grasp,
Love whispers softly, bittersweet.

Spectrum of Sensation

In twilight whispers, colors blend,
Soft murmurs of the day's sweet end.
A canvas swells with secret hues,
Each stroke a world, it's ours to choose.

The scent of rain, a vibrant call,
A soothing balm, embracing all.
In every heartbeat, notes arise,
A symphony 'neath endless skies.

Echoes dance in fields of light,
As shadows stretch and fade from sight.
With every breath, the senses wake,
Creating beauty in our wake.

Through laughter shared, our spirits soar,
In every moment, we explore.
A palette rich, emotions swell,
In this vast universe, we dwell.

Glimmers of joy, soft whispers sigh,
In every glance, we learn to fly.
Embodying love, painted bright,
Through the spectrum, hearts ignite.

Palette of the Soul

A dance of colors, bold and bright,
Each shade a story, dreams take flight.
With every brush, our tales unfold,
In pigments pure, the heart is bold.

Soft pastels of a morning glow,
Crimson whispers, fiery flow.
The canvas breathes with every beat,
In strokes of passion, life is sweet.

Serene blues in twilight's grace,
Colors merge in a warm embrace.
Each hue reflecting journeys made,
In vibrant tones, our fears do fade.

Emerald greens of nature's heart,
In every shade, a brand new start.
Through swirling chaos, we discover,
The masterpiece that lies as cover.

As evening falls, the colors blend,
In every heartbeat, love transcends.
Soul's palette filled with hues so bright,
A world alive in endless light.

Vibrant Odyssey

Each dawn awakens a journey grand,
With vibrant stories across the land.
Adventures beckon, hearts alight,
In every moment, pure delight.

A river's flow, a whispering breeze,
Embracing nature, hearts find ease.
Exploring valleys, mountains tall,
In vibrant hues, we find our all.

With every step, the world unfolds,
In tales of wonder, life retold.
Through laughter shared, tears may fall,
Yet in each moment, we stand tall.

As night descends, the stars ignite,
Guiding our dreams with silver light.
Navigating through the cosmic sea,
An odyssey of you and me.

In every heartbeat, journeys spun,
In vibrant echoes, we are one.
Through every dawn, the stories rise,
Vibrant odyssey beneath the skies.

Tints of Temptation

A gentle brush, the colors sway,
In hues that beckon, night and day.
Soft shades of passion, deep and bright,
In tints of temptation, pure delight.

Whispers of blush in twilight's glow,
With every look, the feelings grow.
Enchanting colors softly tease,
In every moment, hearts find ease.

Golden glimmers where shadows play,
Tempting paths that drift away.
In every breath, a world awaits,
In tints of love, we find our fates.

Crimson kisses, sweet and bold,
In whispered secrets, we unfold.
Through swirling shades, desire sways,
In fleeting hours, love always stays.

Emerald dreams, vibrant and rare,
With every heartbeat, we declare.
In tints of temptation, hearts unite,
A canvas painted with pure light.

Midnight Bloom

Under the moon's soft silver light,
Petals whisper secrets of the night.
In shadows deep, their fragrance swells,
As echoing quiet, a story tells.

Stars twinkle high in the velvet dome,
Nature's canvas, a secret home.
Among the thorns, a beauty rare,
A midnight bloom beyond compare.

Crickets sing in harmonious grace,
As night waltzes in a gentle embrace.
With every gust, a sweet perfume,
Unfolding dreams in the midnight bloom.

Fleeting moments sweep through the air,
Each one cherished, every heart laid bare.
In this hour, time seems to pause,
A perfect world without a cause.

So let us linger 'neath this sky,
And in the magic, hold our sigh.
For in the dark, love's fire will loom,
Together forever, in midnight bloom.

Vortex of Emotion

Spirals of feeling ebb and flow,
A tempest brewing, a silent show.
In shadows and light, they twist and twine,
An ocean of whispers, yours and mine.

With every heartbeat, we rise and fall,
In the dance of fate, we heed the call.
Joy and sorrow, a balanced thread,
In the tapestry woven, our spirits fed.

Conflicting colors bleed and blend,
A spectrum of stories that never end.
Caught in the swirl, we lose our way,
Yet find ourselves in the chaos, they say.

Glimmering moments, both sharp and sweet,
Resonating harmonies of heartbeats meet.
A vortex of emotions, wild and grand,
Where love and pain gracefully stand.

In the eye of the storm, we learn to dance,
Caught in the rhythm of fate and chance.
Through the whirlpool, we dare to feel,
Embracing the truth that makes us real.

Splashing Stardust

Across the sky, the stars ignite,
A sprinkle of magic in the night.
Like diamonds tossed from a celestial hand,
Splashing stardust over the land.

With every shimmer, a dream takes flight,
Guided by the glow of the moon's soft light.
In a whirl of wonder, hopes arise,
As constellations paint the skies.

We reach for sparks that twinkle bright,
As galaxies dance in the velvet night.
Timeless whispers of dreams unspooled,
In the cosmic ocean where hearts are ruled.

Moments of bliss drift on night's sigh,
Bathing in glory as the world goes by.
In this stardust, we shimmer and glow,
In the universe of the lives we sew.

So let us splash in this celestial sea,
With starlit dreams, forever free.
For in the night, our spirits align,
Splashing stardust, truly divine.

Tinted Memories

Faded photographs in an old frame,
Whispered glances of love's sweet flame.
Each color muted, yet vibrant still,
A tapestry of time, a heart's will.

In laughter and tears, the past unfolds,
Stories of heartbeats and hands that hold.
Painted in hues of twilight's glow,
Stories of joy, and some of woe.

Moments captured, a fleeting muse,
Fragrant echoes in the paths we choose.
Each memory tinged with golden light,
A guiding star in the vast night.

We tread softly on the trails we paved,
In every heartbeat, new dreams are saved.
Tinted with love, a gentle embrace,
Breath of nostalgia, life's tender grace.

So hold these memories close to your heart,
For they shape who we are, our lasting art.
In every color that time bestows,
Tinted memories, the sweetest prose.

Melodies on Canvas

Brush strokes dance in vibrant hues,
The canvas sings with shades of blue.
Notes of yellow, orange, and red,
Whispers of stories, waiting to spread.

Each layer tells a tale so bright,
Captured in color, pure delight.
Harmony flows from each swipe and swirl,
A symphony painted, a dream unfurl.

Brush and melody intertwine,
Creating a world where colors align.
In every corner, a song takes flight,
Canvas alive in radiant light.

The artist smiles, heart open wide,
In this vivid realm, worries subside.
Melodies echo, as shadows play,
A canvas where dreams find their way.

Whispered Tints

Softly the colors begin to blend,
Whispers of life in every bend.
Pastels flutter like gentle sighs,
Blushing skies where serenity lies.

Shades of lavender kiss the ground,
A tranquil dance, a soothing sound.
Whispers of green caress the trees,
Nature's palette, a soothing breeze.

Delicate strokes in quiet grace,
Light and shadows find their place.
Each hue murmurs, a story unfolds,
In whispered tints, the heart beholds.

The silence speaks in a colorful way,
A canvas where dreams play.
With every tint, a thought ignites,
Awakening worlds in gentle nights.

Dusting the Horizon

The sun dips low, dust on the rise,
Painting warmth across the skies.
Golden rays touch every crest,
A moment captured, time at rest.

Clouds blush softly, shades of rose,
Whispers of day in evening's prose.
Silhouettes dance where shadows meet,
Horizons dusted with dreams so sweet.

Colors blend in a tender embrace,
Nature's artistry, a tranquil space.
As the day ends, hopes take flight,
In the dust of the horizon, pure delight.

The stars begin their gentle tease,
A canvas of wonder, hearts at ease.
In each glimmer, a story waits,
Dusting horizons, opening gates.

Mosaic of Wishes

Fragments of dreams in colors bright,
A mosaic of wishes, pure delight.
Each piece glimmers with stories untold,
Crafted with care, a sight to behold.

Scattered hopes in vibrant display,
Patterns emerge in a beautiful way.
Unity found in every shard,
A tapestry woven with hearts unguarded.

Every wish, a tile, a spark,
Lighting the path in shadows dark.
Together they form a radiant scheme,
A mosaic of wishes, a shared dream.

In the stillness, they gently gleam,
Whispering secrets of every dream.
Embracing light, they brightly shine,
A mosaic of wishes, truly divine.

Crimson Whispers

In twilight's haze, secrets bloom,
Crimson petals kiss the gloom.
Silent whispers in the air,
Love's soft promise, always rare.

Stars above, like watchful eyes,
Glimmer softly, hear our sighs.
Heartbeats echo, soft and clear,
Crimson whispers drawing near.

Moonlight dances on the ground,
In its glow, lost souls are found.
Every shadow, a tender trace,
In the night, we find our place.

Beneath the sky, our dreams take flight,
Wrapped in warmth, a sweet delight.
Crimson threads weave through the dark,
In this tapestry, love leaves a mark.

As dawn approaches, colors blend,
Each moment cherished, no end.
In the silence, hearts entwine,
Crimson whispers, forever mine.

Canvas of Desire

Upon the canvas, colors swell,
Each stroke a tale, a secret spell.
With vibrant hues, passions collide,
In the art of love, we confide.

Brush in hand, I trace your face,
Each line an echo of time and space.
With every shade, my heart ignites,
In this masterpiece, soul ignites.

Textures blend, emotions soar,
Desire's dance opens the door.
In every curve, a promise lies,
A canvas bright beneath the skies.

Palette spills, a wild embrace,
Lost in shades, we find our place.
With every splash, the world fades,
In this haven, love cascades.

As the final stroke is drawn,
A tapestry of dusk till dawn.
Our hearts imprinted, never shy,
On this canvas, we will fly.

Vivid Embers

In twilight's glow, fires ignite,
Vivid embers dance with light.
Flickering dreams in the dark,
A glowing heart, a tender spark.

Soft whispers carried on the breeze,
With every breath, time seems to freeze.
In the warmth, our shadows play,
Embers flicker, leading the way.

Close your eyes, let moments blend,
In these embers, time suspend.
Heat of passion, fierce and bright,
Guiding us through endless night.

With every crackle, a story told,
Of desires deep, and hearts so bold.
In the silence, souls entwine,
Vivid embers, forever shine.

As dawn breaks, light's gentle hum,
These vivid embers, they'll succumb.
Yet in the heart, they brightly stay,
A fire within will find its way.

The Brush of Longing

A gentle touch, a fleeting brush,
In this moment, hearts feel the rush.
Longing spills like morning dew,
Awakening dreams, fresh and new.

Every glance, a stroke of fate,
Painting love, we celebrate.
With whispers soft as summer rain,
Together, we break every chain.

Fingers trace the paths we've made,
In the shadows, fears allayed.
With every heartbeat, distance fades,
The brush of longing never strayed.

In quiet hours, our spirits soar,
Boundless realms we can explore.
Through valleys deep and mountains high,
With each brush, we touch the sky.

As dusk descends, we hold it tight,
In every color, pure delight.
With brush in hand, our dreams belong,
In every stroke, the brush of longing.

Chasing Rainbows

In the sky where colors blend,
A bridge to dreams, we ascend.
With each step, the hues we trace,
A fleeting glimpse of nature's grace.

Through the mist, a promise shines,
Whispers sweet in gentle lines.
We chase the glow, hand in hand,
Together, in this vibrant land.

Clouds above, they drift and sway,
Guiding us along the way.
With every turn, the spectrum flows,
A journey where the wonder grows.

Beneath the arch, our spirits soar,
Finding treasures, seeking more.
In the light where shadows meet,
We dance in rain, our hearts complete.

So let us venture, brave and bold,
For magic lives in stories told.
Chasing rainbows, high and bright,
In the colors of delight.

Stroke of Fate

In the quiet of the night,
Dreams unfurl, take swift flight.
Paths entwined by fortune's thread,
Whispers linger, hopes widespread.

Choices made, a journey vast,
Moments fleeting, shadows cast.
What we seek may come to find,
As hearts awaken, souls aligned.

Every heartbeat, every chance,
Life a vivid, timeless dance.
With every stroke, the canvas swells,
In fate's embrace, our story dwells.

Wounds may heal, and bridges mend,
A cycle deep, with no end.
In the tapestry we weave,
A beautiful tale, we believe.

So trust the road, let courage bloom,
In every space, in every room.
For in the world of dreams await,
A magic touch, a stroke of fate.

Patterns of Passion

Intricate webs of heart's desire,
Patterns woven, set afire.
From the depth, where feelings rise,
Love unfolds beneath the skies.

Whispers soft, a tender touch,
In these moments, we feel so much.
Every glance, a silent song,
In this rhythm, we belong.

Promises etched in starlit night,
Guiding us towards the light.
With fervor bold, we dare to weave,
A tapestry only we perceive.

Through the chaos, hearts unite,
Drawing strength from shared delight.
In the patterns, love's refrain,
We find our joy, we bear the pain.

So let us dance in sweet embrace,
In the patterns of love's grace.
With every thread, our spirits rise,
In passion's art, our souls entwine.

Blazing Colors

A sunset paints the world anew,
In blazing colors, bright and true.
Flames of orange, tips of gold,
Nature's palette, brave and bold.

Each hue dances, plays with light,
Filling hearts with pure delight.
In the canvas of the day,
Life awakes in splendid play.

Brush the sky with shades divine,
Every moment, an artful line.
Colors clash but find their peace,
In every stroke, our spirits cease.

Through the storm, the vibrant hues,
A promise kept in morning dew.
With every dawn, a fresh reprise,
Where blazing colors harmonize.

So let us bask in radiant rays,
Celebrate these fleeting days.
For in the colors, we shall see,
The brilliance of eternity.

Threads of Ecstasy

In twilight's hush, we weave our dreams,
Through silken strands, each one redeems.
With whispers soft, our hearts entwined,
In this sweet dance, our souls aligned.

The stars above, they shimmer bright,
Like treasures found in the depth of night.
With every breath, we chase the flame,
In ecstasy, we lose our name.

A tapestry spun from passions bold,
In colors rich, our stories told.
We chase the shadows, we seek the light,
In threads of joy, our hearts take flight.

With laughter clear, we break the dawn,
In every touch, a new bond drawn.
Through fleeting moments, forever stays,
In this embrace, we find our ways.

As daylight fades and night appears,
We cherish all, we shed our fears.
In threads of love, we find our grace,
In ecstasy's arms, our rightful place.

Melodies of the Mind

In quietude, the thoughts arise,
Like gentle waves beneath clear skies.
Each note weaves through the air so light,
A symphony born from the night.

The whispers of the soul, they sing,
In harmony, they softly cling.
With every turn, new tales are spun,
In melodies, our lives are one.

A dance of echoes, bright and bold,
Through whispered dreams, our stories unfold.
Each heartbeat plays its unique part,
In the music that fills the heart.

With every sigh and every breath,
The tunes of joy defy sweet death.
In puzzling paths, we stroll along,
In our minds, we find the song.

As twilight casts its golden hue,
The melodies take on a new view.
In stillness deep, the mind reveals,
The truth within, the heart it heals.

Colors of Intensity

With vivid hues, the world ignites,
In every shade, our passion fights.
The reds of love, the blues of pain,
In colors bright, our lives remain.

On canvas vast, we stroke the night,
With fervent dreams, we chase the light.
The greens of growth, the golds of grace,
In pigments rich, we find our place.

With every splash, the heart speaks loud,
In vibrant whispers, we feel proud.
The purples deep, the whites of peace,
In this wild dance, we find release.

Through every brush, the story flows,
In colors bright, the spirit glows.
A tapestry formed with every tear,
In intensity, we conquer fear.

As dawn unfolds, the palette sings,
In vivid dreams, our spirit clings.
We paint our lives, both dark and bright,
In the colors of passion, we take flight.

Lustrous Legacies

In shadows deep, our stories weave,
Through echoes lost, we still believe.
With every step, the past we trace,
In lustrous legacies of grace.

The tales of old, like stars, they glow,
Through whispered winds, their secrets flow.
With hearts on fire, we carry forth,
In every tale, we find our worth.

A legacy built on dreams and tears,
In every pulse, we face our fears.
With courage strong, we write anew,
In this vast world, our spirits grew.

As time unfolds, the shadows play,
In echoes past, we find our way.
With each heartbeat, we honor the night,
In lustrous legacies, we ignite.

With every dawn, the future gleams,
In every echo, our hope redeems.
Through love and loss, we boldly roam,
In lustrous paths, we find our home.

Milton Keynes UK
Ingram Content Group UK Ltd.
UKHW022018230824
447344UK00012B/744

9 789916 870877